D1621900

TABLE OF CONTENTS

Introduction

The Spirit of the Lord is upon me,
because he has anointed me to preach good news to the poor.
He has sent me to proclaim release to the captives
and recovery of sight to the blind,
to set at liberty those who are oppressed,
to proclaim the acceptable year of the Lord.

LUKE 4:18–19

T he Church today is steeped in the experience of being a "field hospital" (see "A Big Heart Open to God," *America Magazine*, Sept. 19, 2013). Unfortunately, there are many wounded and too few caregivers—a new and troubling take on Jesus' words that "the harvest is plentiful but the laborers are few" (Mt 9:37). The wounded include those who, at the epicenter of this tragedy, have been the victims of clergy abuse and the many misguided efforts to cover it up. Moving outward from the center, such scandals have gripped the rest of the body of Christ (1 Cor 12:27), which, most certainly, suffers in solidarity. While penance and prayer are always needed and have their place in the process of reuniting and healing the Church, the time has come for clergy and laity, together, to take more proactive steps.

The Wounded Body of Christ is one such step. The purpose of these adult faith formation materials is fourfold: (1) to engage, through education and faith sharing, adult Catholics whose faith has been challenged by the presence and effect of clergy abuse in the Church; (2) to provide an opportunity for the Church (at all levels) to discuss clergy abuse in a constructive, reflective, and prayerful manner; (3) to high-

The

WOUNDED BODY OF CHRIST

A Parish Group Discussion Guide on Abuse in the Catholic Church

MATTHEW W. HALBACH, PH.D.

TWENTY-THIRD PUBLICATIONS
twentythirdpublications.com

TWENTY-THIRD PUBLICATIONS
One Montauk Avenue, Suite 200
New London, CT 06320
(860) 437-3012 or (800) 321-0411
www.twentythirdpublications.com

ISBN: 978-1-62785-437-5
Printed in the U.S.A.

 A division of Bayard, Inc.

light the call for justice and mercy-making as necessary agents in healing; (4) to solicit new ideas and means of protecting the body of Christ from future abuse and to share this feedback with appropriate local and national leadership.

Session One acknowledges and explores the reality that Christ's body, the Church, is one body with many members. Clerical abuse and its cover-up have wounded this body, the result of which is a shared sense of shame and mistrust that leadership must address, accept accountability, and atone for. This session encourages constructive sharing of concerns, fears, and sorrows regarding clergy abuse, and seeks to foster a desire for greater engagement between laity and leadership.

Session Two acknowledges and explores the reality that the Church will never be the same again. Because of abuse and its cover-up, every member of Christ's body bears an indelible mark of shame, sorrow, anger, and suspicion. Though our woundedness often makes forgiveness and mercy seem impossible, even unwarranted, this session challenges groups to consider the freedom and healing that come through forgiveness as a necessary step toward personal healing and the healing of the body of Christ.

Session Three acknowledges and explores the relationship between God's justice and mercy. It introduces the biblical vision of justice as rehabilitative, not retributive; and it encourages participants to practice forgiveness, not forgetfulness.

Session Four acknowledges and explores a path toward healing and wholeness through greater transparency and accountability measures. To help foster such measures, this session encourages groups to share their wisdom around what changes they think need to happen, particularly on the local level, and share their ideas/concerns with local leadership (e.g., parish staff, parish clergy, diocesan staff, the bishop).

Part of being a field hospital is meeting people (patients) where they are, meeting them in their woundedness, recognizing our own wounds, and walking together on the path of healing. Penance and prayer are vital components as well. But if we do not talk about clergy abuse together and with leadership—if we do not work together as a body and seek proactive solutions—healing efforts will remain impaired, like a wound that has been dressed without first being cleansed. *The Wounded Body of Christ* is a call and a challenge to all the baptized to join together in this important work of healing.

SMALL GROUP SESSIONS

The Wounded Body of Christ is formatted as four small-group discussion sessions. Each session aims at facilitating constructive discussion and faith sharing around both the reality of clergy abuse and the repeated attempts on the part of leadership to cover it up. The hope is that such discussions may provide needed healing and greater solidarity within the Church, starting at the local level. Although these sessions may provide a cathartic or therapeutic experience for some participants—which is a blessing in itself!—its primary purpose is to be a vehicle for adult faith formation with an aim to accompany those who have been—either directly or indirectly—impacted by clergy abuse and its cover-up.

The format for each session includes an opening prayer, Scripture passage and reflection, questions for discussion, and a closing prayer. The time allotment for each session is 60–90 minutes. Meeting frequency is dependent upon availability and interest level, though not staggering the meetings too much is a good rule of thumb.

Each session should include a skilled facilitator. For this topic, a layperson is preferred, although a trusted member of the clergy or another institutional leader may be acceptable. The facilitator will lead the group in prayer, guide the conversation, and establish ground rules for discussion (e.g., respect each participant's viewpoint, refrain from interruptions, encourage but don't force participation from the entire group, etc.).

It is important that these "grass roots"/small group discussions at the local level have an influence on local (diocesan) and national (USCCB) leadership. However, sharing feedback from these discussions with leadership is a sensitive issue. How and what to share, and the level of confidentiality and anonymity, should be determined and agreed upon by participants from the beginning.

The purpose of these discussions is not to identify victims or particular persons in general. Rather, the purpose is faith formation, healing, and providing feedback to leadership so they may have a sense of the local church/institution's practical and spiritual concerns and needs, as well as suggestions for moving forward. With this in mind, facilitators should work with participants who are willing to share their stories/suggestions so that such information is communicated to leadership in an agreed upon and appropriate way. *It is important that the Church be heard!*

In preparation for the first group session (and in times between sessions), all participants are invited to pray and reflect on the following prayer for healing.

A PRAYER FOR HEALING

O Lord, my heart is aching and my spirit is heavy as I consider my own woundedness and the woundedness of your body, the Church, of which I am a member. As a member of your body, help me to find strength to bear my wounds by gazing upon the wounds of your Son, Jesus—wounds that were shamefully inflicted and unjustly received. Help me, too, to be courageous and full of tenderness as I consider how I might, through my own woundedness, bring about healing and light in this toxic and dark time in the Church.

I know that to love others, and to seek out justice, I must seek, first, your kingdom (Mt 6:33), which pours forth from the heart of your Son, Jesus. This heart was pierced for the salvation of many. By his wounds, we are healed (1 Pet 2:24). Help us work together to cleanse and dress the wounds of your Son, as Mary once did. And may we wait in joyful hope for the coming of the Lord and, with him, the resurrection of our own bodies, which make up the body of Christ, the Church!

Amen.

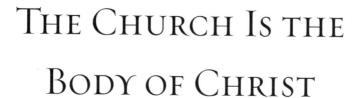

THE CHURCH IS THE BODY OF CHRIST

INTRODUCTIONS

[Facilitator should encourage people to introduce themselves and to share what brought them to this gathering.]

OPENING PRAYER

All: Merciful God, through our meeting together, and by your Holy Spirit, your Son, Jesus Christ, is present with us. Together, may they guide our prayer, reflection, and discussion, that we may give you glory and bring healing to our wounded Church; for we are the body of Christ. If one suffers, we all suffer. We suffer together, and we are saved together. You have called us together, now, to try and live this truth more deeply, and to be a beacon of hope in a time a great darkness. Amen.

Reader: For just as the body is one and has many members, and all the members of the body, though many, are one body, so it is with Christ. For by one Spirit we were all baptized into one body—Jews or Greeks, slaves or free—and all were made to drink of one Spirit. But God has so composed the body, giving the greater honor to the inferior part, that there may be no discord in the body, but that the members may have the same care for one another. If one member suffers, all suffer together; if one member is honored, all rejoice together. Now you are the body of Christ and individually members of it.

The word of the Lord.

All: Thanks be to God.

REFLECTION
The body of Christ is wounded. We are a wounded people.
(JOHN I:I–5; ROMANS I2:4–IO)

[Take turns reading: one reader per paragraph.]
The Church is the body of Christ. Each of us, through baptism, has become a member of this body. As Saint Paul teaches, when one member suffers or rejoices, we are all called to suffer and rejoice together. Clergy abuse (and those who have tried to cover it up) has severely wounded the body of Christ. First and foremost, such abuse and secrecy bring violence and shame to victims. However, clergy abuse has impacted each member of Christ's body, evoking feelings of shame, anger, and despondency in various degrees. So deep is this collective woundedness that many members—both victims and those who empathize with them—are wondering if God still abides with them, individually, and with his Church. Today, many are struggling to rediscover their value and dignity as children of God in the Catholic Church.

By their actions, abusive clergy have caused great division in the body of Christ, beyond a felt disconnect on the part of those who are currently disillusioned with God, who wonder how God could let such things happen. This division is being interpreted by some as a kind of "laity versus clergy" phenomenon, where all clergy are to be viewed with suspicion and treated as potential abusers. How difficult it must be for those who have adopted this view to remain in the Church! How difficult it must be to be a priest or bishop today and be looked upon with such suspicion. So many prayers need to be offered. So many conversations and conversions need to occur. So many new and daring decisions need to be made at leadership levels to make this divided body whole again.

Healing begins with humility. As the *Catechism of the Catholic Church* (CCC) teaches, all of us carry the potential for great evil within ourselves. This is the unfortunate effect of original sin (CCC, 396–402). We all have the potential to be demonic or divine, satanic or saintly. The violence and shame caused by clergy abuse and its cover-up have led to division, the fruit of which is mistrust and, ultimately, separation. Opposing all division is the Spirit of God, who creates, renews, and unites.

[Pause for a moment before asking the following question.]
How might the Spirit use your voice, your gifts to bring about greater peace and understanding during this difficult time in the Church?

During this time of great sorrow and shame, is there another way forward rather than removing ourselves further from the rest of the body of Christ, or demonizing those clergymen who have shown themselves to be more wolf than shepherd? Now is the time to renew our commitment to Christ through a renewed commitment to his entire body—a body that includes both the "sheep" and the "goats" (Mt 25:31–46), the "wheat" and the "chaff," which God, alone, will judge (Mt 3:12). This recommitment includes both a cry for mercy and a call for justice. It involves prayer and action, greater accountability and transparency, and even greater compassion.

[Allow for 5–10 minutes of quiet time before beginning the questions.]

QUESTIONS

1. In what way did the Scripture reading speak to you?
2. What, in the reflection, caught your attention?
3. How has clergy abuse impacted your life, challenged your faith?

CLOSING PRAYER

All: Merciful God, you gave us your Son, Jesus, to be our savior. Through baptism, and in the Holy Spirit, we are united to his body and, therefore, to you. When one of the members of your Son's body suffers, we all suffer. May each member of the body of Christ work toward healing in his or her own way, inspired by the same Spirit who raised Jesus from the dead and descended on the apostles at Pentecost. Holy Spirit, come into each of our lives in a fresh and powerful way, that we may experience the healing we need and share that healing with others.

Amen.

Session Two

BEING A

WOUNDED BODY

OPENING PRAYER

All: Merciful God, you sent your Son to heal and to forgive sins. I need your healing love, both now and always, so that I might find a way to live as a member of your wounded body, the Church. Though I might feel that I cannot trust your ministers, I know I can always trust you. And I know that you still call forth and anoint good people to share your gospel and your grace with others. But I am struggling to live with the shame I feel being a member of your church. The only thing I can cling to is the truth that you have called this church into being, and you will shepherd it into your kingdom. Father, I trust in you. Jesus, I trust in you. Holy Spirit, I trust in you. Amen. [CF. EZEKIEL 34:1–24; PSALM 23; JOHN 10:11–18]

SCRIPTURE (PSALM 10:1–6, 8A–9A, 12–15, 17–18)

Reader: Why, LORD, do you stand far off?

Why do you hide yourself in times of trouble?
In his arrogance the wicked man hunts down the weak,
  who are caught in the schemes he devises.
He boasts about the cravings of his heart;
  he blesses the greedy and reviles the LORD.
In his pride the wicked man does not seek him;
  in all his thoughts there is no room for God.
His ways are always prosperous;
  your laws are rejected by him;
  he sneers at all his enemies.
He says to himself, "Nothing will ever shake me."
  He swears, "No one will ever do me harm."
His eyes watch in secret for his victims;
like a lion in cover he lies in wait.

Arise, LORD! Lift up your hand, O God.
  Do not forget the helpless.
  Why does the wicked man revile God?
  Why does he say to himself,
  "He won't call me to account"?
But you, God, see the trouble of the afflicted;
  you consider their grief and take it in hand.
The victims commit themselves to you;
  you are the helper of the fatherless.
Break the arm of the wicked man;
  call the evildoer to account for his
  wickedness that would not otherwise be
  found out.
You, LORD, hear the desire of the afflicted;
  you encourage them, and you listen to
  their cry, defending the fatherless and the
  oppressed, so that mere earthly mortals
  will never again strike terror.
  The word of the Lord.

All: Thanks be to God.

[This is a powerful psalm! Pause to allow the group to consider a word or phrase from the psalm that might express their own emotions about the abuse scandal. Invite participants to share their word or phrase and why it expresses how they feel.]

REFLECTION
Bearing an indelible mark. God is just and merciful.
(LUKE 15:1–7; JOHN 10:1–18; MATTHEW 5:7; 5:22; 5:29–30;
LUKE 15:11–32; MATTHEW 21:12–17; MATTHEW 23:1–36)

[Take turns reading: one reader per paragraph.]
The Catholic Church today is marked by violations of trust, abuse, and scandal. In a sense, this mark is an indelible one—it cannot be forgotten or removed. It is the opposite of (and opposes) the indelible marks we receive through baptism and confirmation, which are marks of grace, belonging, love, and empowerment that transform us more into the likeness of God. This indelible mark—the mark left by clergy abuse and its cover-up—is a great source of anger and shame in the body of Christ. This anger resounds forcefully with the psalmist who, as one of God's chosen people, is fed up with the abuse of power by the powerful and is demanding that justice be served.

This psalm, like so many others, gives poetic expression to the frustration of Israel who, time and again, has been forced to wait for God to act. Today, the laity feel powerless in the face of the clergy abuse crisis, and the long held belief that change is made from the top down. Some bishops seem so concerned about protecting their institution that they forget to protect their people.

Within these felt constraints, it is tempting to consider taking matters into our own hands, to enact our own plans for justice. But the fruit of revengeful actions only leads to greater injustice and division. If we listen to the psalmist carefully, we will observe that, despite his difficulties, he remains resigned to wait on the Lord to act, for God to exact God's justice. A difficult concept for us, today. To be sure, waiting for God to act is not to advocate for inaction on the part of the Church. Rather, it is to prayerfully (and in discussion with one another) bring our desires for justice to the Lord who purifies our intentions and, in doing so, reveals his course of action.

[Take a moment to reflect on (and share about) the following questions.]
What do you think is the difference between responding and reacting? What is a proper response to the reality that clergy abuse and the attempts to cover it up have been a part of the Church's life for decades?

Jesus is the Good Shepherd who does not want to lose a single sheep, no matter the cost. Yet, at the same time, the gospels reveal Jesus demonstrating righteous anger as he cleanses the temple. Through parable and, sometimes, through more direct language, Jesus teaches his disciples about hell (Gehenna) and everlasting punishment for the unrepentant. These are frightening and incomprehensible possibilities belonging to the justice of God. In fact, the gospels (the good news!) contain the Bible's clearest and most sobering teachings on the terrible and eternal consequences of human choices and actions. Is God just or merciful? The answer is: both.

Although in the gospels mercy and justice seem to be opposed to each other, Jesus represents and brings them together in himself. In his death and resurrection, Jesus demonstrates how divine justice is satisfied through the offering of mercy and grace to all. At times, being merciful seems to go against every logical thought, passion, and bodily impulse. Therefore, we should not be surprised that being merciful is so difficult. To be merciful is to be like Jesus. And it is such a struggle to follow him, to understand and live the awesome and disturbing depths of God's command: to love God and to love one's neighbor as one's self. [CF. DEUTERONOMY 6:4–5; LEVITICUS 19:18; MARK 12:30–31]

[Allow for 5–10 minutes of quiet time before beginning the questions.]

1. How might God be calling you to imitate Jesus today?
   What makes this difficult?
2. How might you channel your righteous anger into something
   life-giving?

CLOSING PRAYER

All: Merciful God, help me to imitate your Son, Jesus, in the manner
you want me to. Only then will I find peace and justice. If I am unable
to pray for God's mercy and share it with others, give me the desire to
do so. May my woundedness and the marks I bear find a home in Jesus'
wounded body. And may my heart remain fixed on the resurrection,
when the body of Christ is raised, wounds and all, to the glory of heav-
en. Amen.

Session Three

Healing a
Wounded Body

OPENING PRAYER

All: Merciful God, mercy is how you show your love for us. You loved us before we knew you. You love us even though we are sinful. You sent your only Son because you love us. There are those in the Church who prefer the darkness to light. Help us to shine the light of your mercy until your entire body of Christ is ablaze for all the world to see! Help us to understand your justice and to trust that your will be done. Amen.

[CF. JOHN 3:19; LUKE 12:49]

SCRIPTURE: (MATTHEW 9:13)

Reader: [And Jesus said:] "But go and learn what this means: 'I desire mercy, not sacrifice.' For I have not come to call the righteous, but sinners."

The word of the Lord.

All: Thanks be to God.

[Pause for a moment of silent reflection before answering the following question:] Besides penance and fasting, what kind of justice and mercy must be shown victims, perpetrators, and concealers of clergy abuse?

REFLECTION

Understanding mercy as God's justice.
Practicing forgiveness but never forgetfulness.

(HOSEA 6:6; JAMES 2:13; MATTHEW 6:15)

[Take turns reading: one reader per paragraph.]

Some people say that the difference between mercy and justice is this: mercy is what we want done to us, and justice is what we want done to everyone else! This view of mercy and justice, while somewhat humorous, is toxic and unbiblical. Yet it seems that many in the body of Christ think along these lines. It is human to want an "eye for an eye" (Ex 21:24); it is natural. It is quite a supernatural thing to pray for our persecutors and to love our enemies (Mt 5:44). But Jesus calls us to do just that. It seems so unfair; and it is…according to our sense of justice, but not according to God's sense of justice. God's ways are not our ways (Is 55:8).

Jesus reveals the truth that God is "just" and "righteous." These two important, biblical words, despite popular usage, do not describe a divine appetite for legalistic justice: "eye for an eye." Rather, they speak to God's humility and to God's longing for a right relationship with humanity and the whole of creation, which is why God's saving plan unfolds the way it does: the Father creates, pronounces creation good, and spares no expense at restoring and renewing creation through the work of the Son and the Spirit (*Catechism of the Catholic Church*, nos. 235, 257–260). There is no doubting, however, the presence of retributive (repayment-type) justice in the Bible. God will allow people who persist in their ways to reap what they sow (Ecc 10:8; Prov 5:22).

Yet Jesus reveals another truth about God: that God is merciful. Scripture abounds with language and examples of God's justice as restorative or rehabilitative. Each miracle of Jesus, for example, demonstrates God's mercy-justice in action. Illness requires a doctor; sin requires a savior. Jesus came to call sinners, not those who already judge themselves righteous—as though they are living in a right relationship with God apart from God's mercy embodied in Jesus. It is not the case that the sick and the sinner *deserve* to be made whole, but that Jesus *longs* for them to be so, to be made "clean" (Mt 8:3).

Jesus calls us to use the power of forgiveness to help us break free of the chains of shame, depression, and self-destructive tendencies, which are often the effects of sin, not to mention abuse. Forgiveness has the power to set the forgiver free. Forgiveness also shifts our perspective. By looking upon one's wrongdoers with pity rather than malice, forgiveness helps forgivers reclaim the dignity that has been robbed from them. People who can forgive begin to remember that they are more than victims; they are people with rights and dignity like everyone else, people who are loved and are capable of loving.

Forgiveness is a graced and daily practice. It is a habit we form. It is work and it is a way of receiving our "daily bread" (Lk 14:4). As we forgive, so are we forgiven. But forgiveness is not the same thing as forgetfulness. Those who have been the victims of clergy abuse will never forget it, nor will they forget the one(s) who did it, or the one(s) who have covered it up. Jesus does not ask us to forget that others have sinned against us. Neither does he want us to forget that we have sinned against others. We ought to keep these moments in mind as a way to protect and guard ourselves from future harm, and as a reminder to avoid harming others in similar ways. We also keep these moments in mind in the hope that we might, one day, empathize with those who harm us, seeing them as they really are: sick and sinful, in need of a physician and a savior. May God's mercy-justice reign over the Church.

[Allow for 5–10 minutes of quiet time before beginning the questions.]

QUESTIONS

1. How have you experienced God's mercy in your life?
2. What kind of mercy might you practice to help the Church heal?
3. What is keeping you from taking the next step toward forgiving those whose abuse has harmed others?

CLOSING PRAYER

All: God, your mercy and justice come together in your Son, Jesus, in a way that highlights your desire to heal and save humanity from its sins. Mercy is a graced action; it is supernatural. To be merciful, we need your help. May the Church begin to heal through a greater outpouring of mercy for victims of abuse and for abusers. May your justice manifest itself in a way that satisfies the deepest desires of the human heart—to be created anew, to be unconditionally loved, and to share this kind of love with others. Amen.

Session Four

ANTICIPATING A GLORIFIED BODY

OPENING PRAYER

All: Merciful God, during this final session, help us to look forward to beholding and being one with the glorified Jesus in heaven. He is our wholeness. May we remember that you make all things new (Rev 21:5), and that nothing is so broken that it cannot be restored. May your Church work to build your kingdom, which is like a beacon on a hill, shining light into the darkness. Darkness, and the secrets that preserve it, have no place in your Church. Your glorified body is a transfigured body, full of light. May we help to preserve the unity of your body, Lord, through collegiality, not clericalism; accountability, not immunity. Amen.

SCRIPTURE (MATTHEW 17:1–2 & LUKE 12:1–3)

Reader: After six days Jesus took with him Peter, James, and John the brother of James, and led them up a high mountain by themselves.

There he was transfigured before them. His face shone like the sun, and his clothes became as white as the light.

[Pause.]

Jesus began to speak first to his disciples: "Beware of the yeast of the Pharisees, which is hypocrisy. There is nothing concealed that will not be disclosed, or hidden that will not be made known. What you have spoken in the dark will be heard in the daylight, and what you have whispered in the inner rooms will be proclaimed from the housetops.
The Gospels of the Lord.

All: Praise to you, Lord Jesus Christ.

[Take a moment to invite sharing around how the previous sessions have impacted participants' thoughts and feelings about the clergy abuse crisis.]

REFLECTION
Moving toward transparency, not secrecy.
Striving for accountability, not clericalism.

[Take turns reading: one reader per paragraph.]
There is little doubt that institutions tend to breed institutionalism: an insulated and defensive posture toward change, criticism and, especially, internal reform. Those in leadership positions tend to maintain the status quo at all costs, often because they feel they are the ones with the most to lose if changes are made. So institutions, if they do change, tend to do so slowly, cautiously. The Catholic Church is no different in this respect. However, in another respect, the Church and other Catholic institutions ought to be and act entirely different from every other institution!

The Church is the body of Christ, made up of people like you and me. It does have institutional and corporate elements to it. But the Church is, first, a body—one that incorporates and brings together many other "bodies" around the world in faith and service to Jesus Christ. The Church ought to change and move at the pace of the body's felt needs. Right now, the body (the Church) is wounded. To varying degrees, every member of the body of Christ has experienced the wounds caused by clerical abuse and its cover-up. And we want to see change!

[Take a moment to invite ideas about what kinds of changes the Church needs to make in light of clergy abuse and its cover-up.]

Underneath this surface layer of institutional reform is the reform needed among the leadership and its constituents. Such reform is more along the lines of personal conversion, including a renewed openness to transparency, to conducting one's self in the light of God and God's people and not in the darkness of secrecy and privilege. In support of this shift, new measures ought to be taken that would make leadership more accountable to the people they serve. In addition, people (e.g., families, people in the pews, volunteers, employees, etc.) must remember that clergy are human beings, capable of both good and evil, people in need of healthy intimacy, and people who need to be held accountable for the sake of the body of Christ and for their own salvation. In the glorified body, there is no room for *clericalism*—the granting of unnecessary and even dangerous privilege and deference to clergy—seeing clergy as unapproachable or infallible. No. The time has come to walk together as Church; to work with and for each other; to love our neighbors as ourselves; to put Christ at the center of our faith and to tend to his wounded body.

There have been many positive steps made at the local church and national levels over the past decades to try and mitigate the potential for clergy abuse. For example, in the U.S., we have The Charter for the Protection of Children and Young People (2002), which laid the ground rules for disciplining abusive clergy; as well as the National Review Board, which advises the bishops' conference on the prevention of sexual abuse of minors. However, we have a long way to go; and it begins with the laity laying hold of their baptismal call to be priest, prophet, and king. Laity must begin to see themselves as gifted, by baptism, with a prophetic voice that clergy need to hear, one that calls them to greater accountability. Some bishops are considering the establishment of lay-led oversight committees for the investigation of alleged abusers in their dioceses. Other bishops, like Archbishop Blase Cupich of Chicago, are calling for the establishment of a lay-led oversight committee for the investigation of bishops accused of clerical abuse.

Moving forward begins when leadership takes a hard look at itself and makes the fundamental option to serve the body of Christ over the status quo, to be transparent, and intentionally discourage the poison of clericalism. Reform begins when everyone, together, believes and lives in anticipation of the glorified body of Christ. We rise and fall together. Our individual salvation is connected to the salvation of every member of the body of Christ and, further reaching, the body of humanity.

[Allow for 5–10 minutes of quiet time before beginning the questions.]

QUESTIONS

1. What can your parish/diocese/bishops' conference do to bring about healing in the Church?
2. What "next steps" can this group propose for ensuring that the insights shared have the possibility for bearing fruit beyond this group setting?

CLOSING PRAYER

A Prayer to the wounded, risen one

All: Lord, you were raised from the dead by the love of the Father and the power of the Spirit. Your body retained the marks of your torture and crucifixion. Yet, they were no longer marks of shame and disgrace, slavery and powerlessness. Now that you that bear these marks while "sitting at the right hand of the power of God" (Lk 22:69), they are given new meaning and purpose. Your marks, your wounds, have become a source of power—the power to reconcile the world to yourself (2 Cor 5:19) and make it whole again. You, who are perfectly complete, made yourself incomplete so that you would be filled and completed by us, the members of your body. Your wounds are signs that the Father has prepared a place for us in you, where we can live forever, whole and held and free. Amen.